Paul Skenes: The Phenom

A Rising Star's Journey From College Ace To MLB Elite

Roman M. Morris

Table Of Contents

INTRODUCTION

Within Major League Baseball's dynamic environment, where dreams come true and legends are made, a new phenomenon has surfaced that is capturing the attention of both fans and analysts. Paul Skenes is a name that conjures images of strength, accuracy, and promise. He rose quickly from being a collegiate ace to an MLB great, changing baseball forever in his wake.

This is a tale of a young man whose journey extends beyond the confines of the baseball pitch; it is a monument to the unflinching quest of success, the unrelenting desire for greatness, and the enormous influence that one person can have on a team, a league, and a future generation of players.

Skenes's climb has been nothing short of remarkable, starting from his early years as a bright prospect in Southern California and continuing through his outstanding undergraduate career at Louisiana State University. He has risen to the top of the baseball world because of his persistent commitment to perfecting his skill, natural athleticism, and intuitive grasp of the game.

Skenes has made a name for himself as one of the game's most exciting pitchers with a fastball that shoots out of his hand like a rocket, a devastating slider that bends knees, and a variety of offerings that keep batters off balance. However, his accomplishments go well beyond his strength. He is respected and admired by both opponents and teammates for his leadership abilities, mental toughness, and unshakeable calm under duress.

Through the captivating trip "Paul Skenes: The Phenom," we learn about the life and career of this rising celebrity. We go into his early years, examining the factors that influenced his love of baseball and his family's steadfast support. We saw his ascent through the collegiate levels, as he broke records and established new benchmarks for performance. We follow him as he makes his way to the Major Leagues, where he has stunned baseball fans and experts alike with his incredible skill.

However, this is more than just an accomplishment and statistical narrative. It's a tale of tenacity, commitment, and unshakeable faith in one's own skills. It is the tale of a young guy who has accepted the difficulties and setbacks that come with competing at the greatest level and has used them as motivation to reach even higher goals.

As we read this biography, we will discover more about the person who is behind the phenomenon and has won the hearts and minds of baseball fans around. We will learn about his interests, his driving forces, and the principles that he lives by both on and off the field.

Come celebrate with us Paul Skenes' incredible journey. He is a rising talent who will have a lasting impact on baseball. This is a narrative that will enthral, uplift, and create a lasting effect on everyone fortunate enough to see his incredible skill.

CHAPTER 1: THE EARLY SPARK

Childhood in Southern California

A young Paul Skenes set out on a path that would eventually take him to the vast stage of Major League Baseball in the sun-drenched heart of Southern California, where dreams blossom beneath an unending blue sky. Skenes was born on May 29, 2002, in the thriving city of Fullerton, California. His early years were tied together by a strong sense of community, family, and an undying love of sports.

Skenes grew up in the charming village of Lake Forest, which is bordered by expansive suburbs and undulating hills. His family was kind and encouraging to him. His parents taught him the virtues of tenacity, discipline, and hard work—qualities that would be helpful to him in

his athletic endeavours. They were also
, passionate sports fans.

Skenes showed an innate talent for athletics at
a young age, dominating a range of sports. He
was an excellent track and field athlete, a
talented basketball player, and a superb soccer
player. But it was baseball that won him over
and stroked his desire to compete.

Skenes' baseball career took off at El Toro
High School, the same institution that turned out
MLB players Nolan Arenado and Matt
Chapman. He demonstrated his abilities as a
pitcher, catcher, first baseman, and third
baseman, demonstrating his versatility as a
player. Coaches and scouts were immediately
drawn to him because of his strong arm and
remarkable bat speed, and they saw that he had
what it took to become something really
exceptional.

Skenes's time in high school was filled with
both academic and athletic success. He kept up a
demanding workout regimen, juggling his
education and baseball commitments, and
developing a close bond with his teammates. In

addition to being a respected member of the community in the classroom, he was a leader on the field.

Outside of sports, Skenes had a regular upbringing in Southern California. He lost numerous hours strolling along the beaches, trekking in the neighbouring mountains, and taking in the sun-kissed way of life that characterises the area. He fell in love with surfing, a passion that he would carry with him for the rest of his life and use as a means of adventure and pleasure.

Growing up in Southern California, Skenes experienced a period of personal development, exploration, and the fostering of a fervent love for baseball. It was a period when he sowed the seeds of his future greatness, which were nourished by a loving family, a thriving neighbourhood, and an unflinching faith in his own skills.

Skenes brought with him the principles his family had ingrained in him, the lessons he had learnt in Southern California, and his unshakeable will to fulfil his ambitions as he readied himself to start the next chapter of his adventure. He now had the groundwork in place for an incredible career that would take him all the way to the top of professional baseball.

Family Influences and Athletic Upbringing

In the close-knit Skenes family, sports were a way of life rather than just a hobby. Craig and Karen, Paul's parents, were both former athletes. Because Craig played baseball at the Air Force Academy, his kid developed an early passion for the game. Karen, a former Cal Poly Pomona volleyball player, emphasised the value of commitment and cooperation.

Sportsmanship, diligence, and tenacity were valued highly in the Skenes family atmosphere. Over dinner, talk would often turn to training methods, game plans, and the mental toughness needed to succeed in any sport. Sean, Paul's elder brother and a skilled water polo player, was a friendly opponent as well as a role model. The competitive nature of the siblings encouraged one another to always do better and aim higher.

The Skenes family valued education just as much as athletic endeavours, but they never overlooked the former. Paul was pushed to do well in school while juggling his growing sports career and his academic obligations. He developed a strong work ethic and efficient time management abilities as a result of this dual concentration, which would come in very handy as he advanced in his baseball career.

Sports played a major part in their life, as shown by the fact that family trips were often planned around sports events. The Skenes family made a lot of experiences together via their love of sports, whether it was playing catch in the backyard, going to MLB games, or watching collegiate competitions.

Outside of the immediate family, Paul's athletic background was greatly influenced by the Skenes' close friends and extended family. They never wavered in their support, showing up to his games, encouraging him from the sidelines, and giving him words of wisdom both in the wind and the loss. This support system fostered a caring atmosphere that facilitated Paul's growth as a person and an athlete.

Paul's skill flourished because of the Skenes family's focus on athletics and their constant support and encouragement. His love for baseball was sparked, his abilities were refined, and his will to achieve was cemented in this supportive atmosphere. His incredible path to the top of professional baseball would be built on the teachings he received from his family, both on and off the field.

Finding Passion for Baseball

Baseball wasn't just a pastime to young Paul Skenes; it was an awakening and the source of a passion that would change the course of his life. Growing up in Southern California, where baseball is a major sport, one cannot avoid the sport's influence. Paul's mind was captivated by the sounds of the game, including the crack of the bat, the roar of the audience, and the legends of the great players.

Initially, baseball was just a pastime and a means of strengthening his bonds with his brother and father. They would play catch, whack balls, and act like their favourite MLB players for endless hours in the backyard. Paul's first encounters kindled an interest in the sport, prompting him to delve more into it.

Paul's obsession with baseball developed as he got older. He was enthralled with the agility, strategy, and sheer drama that transpired on the field while he watched games on television. He started learning about the subtleties of the game, including various pitches, defensive alignments, and offensive tactics. Posters of his favourite baseball players covered the walls of his bedroom, acting as a continuous reminder of his goals.

Paul loved baseball, and he played it outside the house. He signed up for Little League teams, excited to play against other young kids and participate in training and games. Attending local high school and college games allowed him to fully immerse himself in the sport's culture, taking in the atmosphere and picking the brains of players he looked up to.

As his proficiency increased, so did his passion for the game. He devoted several hours to practise, perfecting his hitting approach, enhancing his defensive abilities, and sharpening his throwing mechanics. Despite his innate athletic ability—a strong arm and a fast bat—what really made him stand out was his constant commitment to and passion for the game.

Paul's passion for baseball extended beyond only the actual act of participating in the game. It was all about the comradery, the feeling of community, and the joint pursuit of a single objective. It was about the exhilaration of winning, the anguish of losing, and the life lessons discovered.

Paul's love for baseball remained unwavering as he advanced through the juvenile divisions.

He accepted the difficulties, the failures, and the victories, constantly aiming to do better and realise his full potential. His passion for baseball had shaped his ideals, ambitions, and future objectives, becoming an essential part of who he was.

It was this persistent devotion that helped Paul Skenes reach the highest level of baseball professionalism. His story, which began when he was a little child playing catch in the backyard and ended when he became a Major League player, is proof of the value of hard work, the ability to follow one's aspirations, and the life-changing effects of true love.

CHAPTER 2: HIGH SCHOOL HEROICS

El Dorado High School: A Star is Born

El Dorado High School, located in the middle of Orange County, California, surrounded by expansive suburbs and brightly lit scenery, provided the perfect setting for Paul Skenes' rise to fame as a baseball player. His amazing skill blossomed inside the hallowed halls of this school, capturing the interest of scouts, coaches, and fans alike.

Skenes was unmistakable as soon as he walked onto the El Dorado baseball pitch. Fastballs were sent towards home plate with incredible velocity by his strong arm, which was developed over many hours of practice and his innate agility. A strong opponent for any hitter, he was intimidating on the mound due to his constant concentration and competitive nature.

Skenes' time in high school was filled with astounding feats of talent and record-breaking achievements. He led his squad to win after victory while routinely dominating opposition lineups, minimising hits, and striking out a high number of batters. Batters were left perplexed and disappointed by his pitching arsenal, which included a lethal slider, a developing changeup, and a blistering fastball.

However, Skenes was not simply a pitcher. He was a real five-tool player, a master of all the game's facets. His ability to bat for average and power demonstrated his offensive brilliance, as he caused havoc on the basepaths and drove balls far into the outfield. Whether he was playing first base, patrolling the hot corner at third, or behind the plate as a catcher, his defensive abilities were equally excellent.

Skenes had a revolutionary effect on the El Dorado baseball program. He led the squad to deep playoff campaigns and league titles by bringing their performance to new heights. His presence on the field motivated his teammates to perform at a higher level and pursue excellence.

In addition to his sporting accomplishments, Skenes was well-liked in the El Dorado neighbourhood. He balanced his sporting responsibilities and maintained a stellar GPA, making him a model student. Along with being a leader in the classroom and halls, he also set an example for his classmates by being modest, sportsmanlike, and hardworking.

During his tenure at El Dorado High School, Skenes had exceptional personal development. He became one of the best high school baseball players in the nation by honing his abilities and improving his strategy. He received several distinctions and trophies for his on-field achievements, including All-State status, league MVP honours, and a berth on the esteemed Perfect Game All-American squad.

As Skenes was ready to graduate from El Dorado, he had a promising future in baseball. He was already set to play collegiately at the Air Force Academy, where he would further his training and aim to become a professional athlete. However, his impact at El Dorado would live on, inspiring next student-athlete generations and acting as a reminder of the value of perseverance, hard effort, and unshakable devotion.

Commitment To The Air Force Academy

A tribute to his multidimensional personality, Paul Skenes' devotion to the Air Force Academy demonstrated not just his physical talent but also his commitment to discipline, duty, and academic accomplishment. His choice was a reflection of his own principles and his desire to follow a career that would push him both on and off the field.

Skenes was attracted to the Air Force Academy's illustrious history of honour, integrity, and leadership from an early age. It was impossible to reject the chance to follow his love of baseball and serve his nation. He saw himself as a cadet who would compete at the top level of college baseball while juggling tough academic work and rigorous military training.

There was doubt and support for Skenes' choice to enrol at the Air Force Academy. Some questioned if his baseball career would suffer as a result of the rigorous schedule of the school, while others applauded his dedication to duty and the unconventional route he had chosen. For Skenes, however, the choice was always obvious. Driven by an uncompromising work ethic and an unchanging will to achieve, he was confident in his talents to flourish in all parts of academy life.

Skenes acclimated himself swiftly to the demanding academic and military milieu of the Air Force Academy in Colorado Springs. Taking on a rigorous curriculum that comprised classes in engineering, aeronautics, and military strategy, he welcomed the difficulties of the classroom. He also engaged in the demanding physical training program at the school, pushing himself to the maximum in both his physical and mental abilities.

Even with the rigorous schedule, Skenes' baseball career was still thriving. He won several honours and recognitions and soon made a name for himself as one of the best pitchers in the Mountain West Conference. The Falcons had unprecedented success because of his outstanding outings on the mound, which included their first NCAA tournament berth in more than 50 years.

Skenes made several sacrifices as part of his dedication to the Air Force Academy. Because of the rigorous rules and rigorous schedule of the school, he had to make tough decisions and give up social chances and personal liberties in order to achieve his objectives. However, he never faltered in his dedication to serving others, embracing the possibilities and trials that came with becoming a cadet.

Skenes' experience at the Air Force Academy was life-changing; it helped him develop into a well-rounded person with a clear sense of purpose and a profound respect for the virtues of leadership, discipline, and service. The experiences and lessons he obtained throughout his time at the school would continue to influence his life and career for years to come, even though his route would eventually take him away from it and into a professional baseball career

Balancing Academics And Athletics

Paul Skenes had a great struggle juggling academics and sports at the Air Force Academy, which is known for its demanding standards in both areas. He did, however, handle this dual road with amazing competence, demonstrating his unshakeable will, methodical approach, and superb time management abilities.

The academic program at the Air Force Academy is renowned for its rigour and covers a broad variety of topics, such as engineering, aeronautics, and military science. High academic standards and adherence to the rigorous military training requirements of the institution are demanded of cadets. There is no room for mistake or procrastination with this rigorous program, so careful preparation and effective time management are required.

Skenes applied the same concentration and effort to his academic work as he did to his performance on the baseball field. He carefully completed homework, engaged in class discussions, and showed up to class every day. To optimise his learning, he made use of all the resources at his disposal, creating study groups and asking instructors and other students for assistance when necessary.

Skenes created a regimented timetable that maximised his productivity and reduced distractions in order to manage his scholastic endeavours and sporting obligations. He spent his mornings studying before practices, his afternoons doing assignments and getting ready for tests, and his intervals between classes going over his notes. Additionally, he learnt to decline social invitations and other interruptions that would cause him to go off course.

Skenes' commitment to his studies went beyond his want to keep his baseball eligibility. He honestly believed that education was important and would help him succeed in life off the field as well. He saw his academic endeavours as a way to increase his knowledge base, hone his critical thinking abilities, and get ready for a job outside of baseball.

His ability to go from the classroom to the baseball field with ease astounded his coaches and teammates. He was a leader in all fields, guiding his colleagues with his unrelenting discipline, devotion to quality, and work ethic. By proving that it was possible to succeed in both academics and athletics, he motivated people around him to pursue excellence in all facets of their life.

Skenes saw the difficulties of juggling academics and sports as a chance for personal development, despite the fact that they were very difficult. He gained knowledge about the value of tenacity, prioritising, and time management. He acquired a solid work ethic, a disciplined way of living, and an unwavering quest for greatness.

Skenes' remarkable character and constant commitment are shown by his ability to juggle studies and sports at the Air Force Academy. It is an incredible accomplishment that has motivated a significant deal of young athletes by showing that excellence can be attained in both the classroom and the sporting arena.

CHAPTER 3: LSU ARRIVAL: A NEW CHAPTER BEGINS

Transfer To Louisiana State University

Paul Skenes made a crucial choice in the summer of 2022 when he moved from the Air Force Academy to Louisiana State University (LSU). This decision would greatly impact his undergraduate baseball career and lay the groundwork for his explosive ascent to professional greatness. This move was a game-changer for Skenes since it gave him fresh opportunities to grow as a pitcher and catapulted him into the public eye.

It was not an easy choice to drop out of the Air Force Academy. Skenes had prospered in the regimented atmosphere of the institution, striking a balance between his scholastic and athletic obligations. But it was too hard to resist the draw of participating in a Power Five conference, which offered more professional scout exposure and a higher level of competitiveness.

With its illustrious baseball history and fervent supporters, LSU offered Skenes a unique chance to display his skills on a larger platform. The Tigers were renowned for their relentless dedication to greatness, their competitive spirit, and their long history of developing players of MLB ability. It was a curriculum that precisely complemented Skenes's own goals and objectives.

There were some difficulties with the transfer procedure. Skenes had to make his way through the NCAA transfer rules in order to be eligible to play right away at LSU. In addition, he had to get used to a new coaching staff, new teammates, and a new academic setting. However, he met these obstacles head-on with his usual tenacity and fortitude, keen to establish himself in his new environment.

As soon as Skenes got to LSU, he made a name for himself as a formidable pitcher. The pitching instructors at LSU helped him improve the velocity and movement of his already potent fastball. His breaking pitch, a lethal slider, sharpened and became even more elusive. He was able to routinely challenge batters and rack up strikeouts because of his better command of the strike zone.

Skenes had an instant and significant influence on the LSU baseball program. He developed into the pitching staff's ace, helping the Tigers win a lot of games and go far in the College World Series. His accomplishments on the mound brought him national attention, which culminated in his receipt of the esteemed Dick Howser Trophy, which is presented to the nation's best college baseball player each year.

Skenes' career turned out to be a turning point when he transferred to LSU. It gave him the stage and the means to completely realise his potential and cultivate his gifts. He was forced to improve and develop into a more complete pitcher as a result of being exposed to a better calibre of competition. In addition, it elevated him to a national level of recognition, drawing the interest of MLB scouts and reaffirming his position as one of the best prospects in the next draft.

Looking back, Skenes' choice to transfer to LSU was a brilliant one, a well-thought-out action that helped him reach new heights and laid the groundwork for his quick ascent to professional superstardom. It was evidence of his drive for success, his unflinching faith in his skills, and his desire.

Adjusting To College Baseball

Paul Skenes' voyage to Louisiana State University (LSU) to play collegiate baseball was characterised by his quick development, adaptability, and the birth of a tremendous talent. Even though he was a highly anticipated talent when he joined LSU, the transition from high school to the Southeastern Conference (SEC), which is known for its intense competitiveness and great pitching, brought with it its own set of difficulties.

At first, Skenes had to deal with the expected transition phase that many inexperienced pitchers have when they play collegiate ball. College batters need a higher degree of accuracy and control because of their high speed and sophisticated approach. He was inconsistent in his early appearances as he struggled to control his natural power and improve the pitch he chose.

But Skenes's drive and work ethic were immediately apparent. He listened to the coaching staff at LSU and studied his mechanics and pitch sequencing in great detail. He put in endless hours honing his craft in the bullpen, experimenting with grips and release positions. This commitment to progress started to show benefits very soon.

Skenes improved his command and control, which was one of his biggest changes. Although he had always had a strong fastball, he was able to pinpoint its location more precisely, which allowed him to hit his spots and keep batters off balance. Additionally, he gained a more sophisticated grasp of pitch sequencing, positioning himself to take advantage of hitters' vulnerabilities with his slider and changeup after setting them up with his fastball.

Skenes' mental approach to the game was an important part of his progress. Pitching in the SEC came with higher expectations, and he had to learn how to handle that pressure. He established a pre-game ritual that helped him concentrate and approach each start with clarity. Despite his youth, he radiated calm assurance on the pitch, remaining composed even under duress.

Skencs's changes were more noticeable as the season went on. His strikeout totals skyrocketed as his ERA gradually dropped. From being a bright prospect, he became a dominating force in the LSU rotation. His ability to command his fastball with precise precision made it even more lethal than it already was. His slider became a genuine out pitch that could produce swings and misses at any stage of the count.

Beyond the statistical gains, there was a discernible change in Skenes' general attitude when pitching. His increasing self-assurance and swagger were evidence of his diligence and hard work. He accepted the leadership position that his success inevitably brought, becoming a respected figure in the LSU clubhouse and a force to be heard on the mound.

Skenes had not only adapted to collegiate baseball by the conclusion of his first season at LSU, but had flourished in it. He made a name for himself as one of the best young pitchers in the country and won honours and recognition for his exceptional play. His achievements were a result of his innate ability, his unshakable work ethic, and the priceless advice he got from the LSU coaching staff.

Paul Skenes' tale of resiliency, flexibility, and enormous potential fulfilment was his transition to collegiate baseball. He took on the difficulties head-on, welcomed the process of learning, and became a dominating force in one of the collegiate baseball world's most competitive conferences. His story is an encouragement to young athletes worldwide, showing that even the most difficult adjustments can be successfully handled with perseverance, hard effort, devotion, and a readiness to learn.

CHAPTER 4 : COLLEGE DOMINANCE: RECORD-SETTING PERFORMANCES

Sophomore Breakout Season

Paul Skenes had an incredible sophomore season at Louisiana State University (LSU), which was a turning point in his developing baseball career. Skenes was already regarded as a potential prospect going into the 2023 campaign, but his sophomore season performance exceeded all predictions and cemented his place among the country's best college pitchers.

Skenes assumed a key position in LSU's pitching rotation for the 2023 season, a duty he accepted with amazing grace and maturity. Already a formidable weapon, his fastball gained even more velocity, often hitting in the high nineties and sometimes even reaching triple digits. With better movement and command, this increased velocity made his fastball almost unhittable for opposing hitters.

But Skenes' supremacy went much beyond his lightning-fast fastball. His deadly slider, which baffled batters with its late action and crisp break, became his go-to weapon in pivotal moments. Although he didn't use it as often, his changeup was a useful third pitch that kept hitters off balance and guessing.

Skenes had a strong variety of pitches, he was a terror for opposing teams on the mound because of his unrelenting resolve and poise, as well as his 6'6" stature and muscular build, which enabled him to create enormous force behind his deliveries.

Skenes' numbers became better as the season went on, and it was obvious how dominant he was. He produced quality starts on a regular basis, striking out batters at a remarkable clip, and keeping his ERA among the lowest in the nation. His reputation as a clutch player was further cemented by his capacity to perform well under duress in high-stakes games.

Skenes' outstanding season earned him a lot of honours and acclaim, including a spot among collegiate baseball's best pitchers. Because of his outstanding performance, he was recognized nationally and selected to many All-American teams. His efforts were crucial to LSU's success all season long, as the squad was always regarded as one of the best in the country.

Beyond his statistical successes, Skenes' sophomore year was distinguished by his increasing maturity and self-assurance as a pitcher. He showed a thorough comprehension of his trade by being able to modify his strategy in response to the game's circumstances and the opposing hitters. As he established himself as a respected figure in the LSU clubhouse and as a loud presence on the mound, his leadership abilities also started to show.

Paul Skenes' second year at LSU was a breakthrough year. His outstanding play, characterised by a potent fastball, enhanced secondary pitches, and steady poise, catapulted him to the top of the collegiate baseball ranks. In addition to being well-known among baseball fans, he cemented his place among the top prospects in the approaching MLB draft. In addition to showcasing his extraordinary skill, his sophomore season also showed signs of his ability to become a formidable force in the professional ranks.

Junior Year: Acknowledgment on a National Level

During his junior year at Louisiana State University (LSU), Paul Skenes achieved unprecedented dominance, garnered national attention, and quickly rose to the top of the collegiate baseball ranks. With a blend of raw power, unshakable competitive spirit, and perfect accuracy, he captivated both fans and experts with a performance on the mound that went beyond simple numbers.

It was clear from the beginning of the 2023 season how dominant Skenes was. He often put on thrilling performances, putting opponents out of their misery with a slider that defied contact and a fastball that hit triple digits. He was able to regularly paint the edges of the strike zone and keep batters off balance because of his extraordinary command of both pitches.

Skenes' stats increased to previously unheard-of levels throughout the course of the season. In addition to having one of the lowest ERAs in the country, he led the country in walks and hits per inning pitched (WHIP), strikeouts, and strikeouts per nine innings. He often pitched far into games, giving LSU a dependable and commanding presence in the circle.

Skenes' outstanding performance won him significant acclaim throughout the country. Consensus All-American is a distinguished title given to the greatest collegiate baseball players, and he received it. Additionally, he was the recipient of various weekly and monthly accolades, including multiple Collegiate

Baseball Journal National Player of the Week honours.

Among the greatest honours Skenes was given was the coveted Dick Howser Trophy, which is given to the best collegiate baseball player each year. His reputation as one of the most influential and dominating athletes in sports history was solidified by this accolade. In addition, he was recognized as a very exceptional pitcher by Collegiate Baseball with the National Pitcher of the Year title.

Skenes' influence went beyond winning specific accolades. He was a key component of LSU's season-long success, helping the club to a deep playoff run and College World Series participation. He was a genuine game-changer for the Tigers because of his capacity to produce clutch performances under duress.

Skenes won over fans and commentators with his humility, hard ethic, and love of the game in addition to his accomplishments on the field. He avoided acknowledgment and emphasised the value of teamwork by always attributing his accomplishments to his mentors and teammates.

He was an inspiration to young athletes because of his unwavering pursuit of perfection and commitment to lifelong growth.

The highlight of Skenes' junior year came when the Pittsburgh Pirates picked him as the first overall choice in the 2023 MLB draft, creating history. This accomplishment was the result of years of perseverance, hard effort, and faith in his own ability. As he started his trip to the big leagues, it also marked the start of a new chapter in his career.

It was a season of unmatched domination, national attention, and a quick ascent to the top of collegiate baseball for Paul Skenes. Fans and commentators alike were enthralled by his extraordinary skill, unrelenting work ethic, and modest manner, which elevated him to the status of one of the most renowned and revered athletes in sports history. His junior year served as a turning point in his career and served as evidence of his tremendous talent and relentless quest of perfection.

Awards And Accolades

Paul Skenes has amassed an impressive array of awards and accolades demonstrating his extraordinary skill, domination on the mound, and overall effect on the game throughout his time as a college student and beginning his professional baseball career.

College Career:

2021

- First Team All-American (Collegiate Baseball Newspaper
- Baseball America, NCBWA)
- Mountain West Conference Freshman of the Year
- National Co-Freshman of the Year

2022:

- John Olerud Award (National two-way player of the year) are

2023:

- Dick Howser Trophy (National Player of the Year)
- Southeastern Conference Pitcher of the Year
- Consensus First Team All-American
- National Pitcher of the Year (Collegiate Baseball Newspaper)
- College World Series Most Outstanding Player
- First Overall Pick (Pittsburgh Pirates) in the MLB Draft

Minor League Career

2023

- Pitcher of the Week (twice) in the Florida State
- Futures Games Selection

Major League Career:

2024:

- MLB All-Star

Skenes has consistently excelled and dominated at every level of competition, as seen by these trophies. His early-career success as a pitcher and hitter won him the coveted John Olerud Award, demonstrating his exceptional two-way abilities. His career took a dramatic turn when he transferred to LSU, where he went on to become one of the most dominating pitchers in collegiate baseball history.

Skenes' remarkable junior campaign resulted in a historic season full of awards, including the highly sought-after Dick Howser Trophy, National Pitcher of the Year, and the title of best player in the College World Series. His ranking as one of the most promising prospects in recent memory was cemented when he was chosen as the first overall choice in the MLB draft.

Skenes' exceptional pitching has earned him acclaim even in his early professional career. He was chosen to play in the esteemed Futures

Game, which features the top young baseball talent, and has received several minor league Pitcher of the Week awards.

In addition to these official honours, Skenes has gotten a lot of unofficial recognition from fans, coaches, teammates, and pundits. He is often complimented for his maturity, work ethic, competitiveness, and leadership abilities. He is an example to ambitious sportsmen because of his capacity to maintain humility and groundedness in the face of incredible success.

Paul Skenes' extensive list of honours and achievements bears witness to his outstanding skill, unwavering commitment, and influence on baseball. It's unlikely that he won't add many more distinguished awards to his already excellent portfolio as he pursues his career. He has a bright future in baseball and is expected to rank among the best pitchers of his age.

The Choice to Become Professional

Paul Skenes' choice to become a professional and declare for the 2023 MLB Draft was a significant turning point in his developing baseball career. It was the result of years of perseverance, hard work, and faith in his own ability. He had to examine a number of variables before deciding to give up his remaining college eligibility at LSU, but eventually, a few important elements drove him to follow his ambition of becoming a professional baseball player.

Skenes surged to the top of the MLB draft boards because of his outstanding performance in his junior year at LSU, when he became one of the most dominating pitchers in college baseball history. He was a very desirable prospect for professional clubs because of his uncommon mix of height, speed, and command. He had the ability to contribute right away at the greatest level.

The monetary rewards that come with being a first-round draft selection surely played a big role in Skenes' choice. He and his family were given the possibility to realise lifetime aspirations and ensure financial stability by obtaining a large signing bonus and maybe earning a sizable income in the big leagues.

Skenes has always been motivated by a strong sense of rivalry and a desire to put himself to the test against the greatest. The temptation of taking against the greatest batters in the world in Major League Baseball offered an unstoppable challenge as well as a chance to hone his abilities and establish himself on the biggest platform.

For Skenes, the 2023 draft's scheduling proved very advantageous. Teams were keen to get a player of his quality since there wasn't a clear-cut, unanimous first choice. It was very tempting to have the chance to perhaps be chosen first overall, which is an uncommon and distinguished award.

Skenes spoke with his advisers, trainers, and family before making his choice. Throughout his time in college, they provided him with invaluable advice and support that eventually aided in his growth and enabled him to make difficult decisions.

Skenes has always dreamed of being a major league baseball player and leaving a lasting impression on the game. He was able to achieve his goals and start a new chapter in his life that was full with chances, challenges, and the possibility of greatness because he had the chance to become pro.

Skenes did not make the choice to become pro lightly, even if it was ultimately his own. He thanked LSU for giving him the chance to play and recognized the vital part the school and its coaching staff had played in his growth. But the opportunity to fulfil his lifetime aspirations and the attraction of professional baseball turned out to be the decisive considerations.

The baseball community reacted enthusiastically and with overwhelming support to Skenes' decision to become pro. Many saw him as having the potential to be a dominating force in the big leagues because of his skill, work ethic, and competitive spirit. His transformation from a bright college prospect to a first-round selection in the draft is evidence of his commitment, tenacity, and unshakable faith in his skills.

Paul Skenes' deliberate decision to become a professional baseball player was motivated by his competitive spirit, goals, and desire to leave a lasting impression on the game. Even though he had to say goodbye to LSU, it was a bittersweet choice that signalled the start of a promising new chapter in his career, one that offered him the chance to excel on the biggest platform.

CHAPTER 5: THE MLB DRAFT: THE PIRATES' PRIZED PICK

Draft Day Drama

There was an exciting undertone of fascination and speculation around Paul Skenes' possible selection in the 2023 MLB Draft leading up to the draft. Even though he was a top prospect due to his extraordinary skill and stellar junior season at LSU, it was still intriguing to wonder whether he would be chosen first overall.

The mystery was that there was no definitive agreement on the best choice. Dylan Crews, Skenes's excellent outfield partner at LSU, was also thought to be a serious candidate for the first overall pick. After showcasing their exceptional skills all season long, the Pittsburgh Pirates who were in possession of the much sought-after first pick had a difficult choice to make.

Baseball fans and members of the media were debating and discussing each player's attributes and making predictions about who would be selected as the draft day drew near. Mock drafts were revised often, with Skenes and Crews frequently trading top spots. As the draft day approached, there was a tangible feeling of excitement and expectation due to the uncertainty.

The fact that Skenes and Crews were close friends in addition to colleagues added to the drama. Together, they had experienced an incredible trip at LSU, where they had led the team to the College World Series and won individual honours. The emotional intricacy of the scenario increased with the possibility that one of them might be chosen before the other.

When the Pittsburgh Pirates took the stage to make their pick on draft day, the suspense peaked. The baseball world held its breath as conjecture and expectation flooded the air. Everyone involved experienced a range of emotions when the Pirates ultimately revealed Paul Skenes as the first overall selection.

It was a moment of validation and victory for Skenes, a result of years of perseverance, hard work, and faith in his own skills. His dream of being selected as the #1 overall choice came true, fulfilling a lifetime goal of becoming a top-tier professional baseball player.

It was a bittersweet time for Crews. He was obviously thrilled for his buddy and teammate, but he also seemed a little disappointed that he wasn't chosen as the winner overall. His sadness was short-lived, however, as the Washington Nationals took him second overall, cemented LSU's legacy as the first college to have two players taken with the first two selections in the MLB Draft.

Paul Skenes' draft day drama was a compelling tale that perfectly encapsulated the spirit of rivalry, friendship, and pursuing one's aspirations. It demonstrated the emotional rollercoaster that athletes and their families go through as well as the unexpected nature of the selection process. Ultimately, the aspirations of

Skenes and Crews to play professional baseball were realised, and their dramatic draft day experience will live on in the annals of baseball history forever.

Signing With The Pittsburgh Pirates

The Pittsburgh Pirates' signing of Paul Skenes was a historic event that signalled the start of a new chapter for the player and the team. Skenes attracted a great deal of interest and was signed to a record-breaking contract as the first overall choice in the 2023 MLB Draft.

Skenes and the Pirates moved quickly and amicably through the negotiations, demonstrating their shared enthusiasm and alignment of objectives. In an attempt to sign the highly anticipated talent, the Pirates extended to Skenes a record-breaking signing bonus of $9.2 million—the largest sum ever given to a draft selection. This exceeded Spencer Torkelson's record-breaking $8.416 million from 2020.

In addition to the sizable signing bonus, Skenes' deal contained a planned compensation plan for his future in the lower levels and maybe the big leagues. Although the wage structure's contents were kept private, it was intended to provide Skenes financial stability and to recognize and reward his accomplishments.

The Pittsburgh Pirates' home field, PNC Park, served as the venue for the formal signing ceremony. Skenes, his family, media representatives, and Pirates officials were present for the occasion. Skenes received his Pirates shirt as a token of his formal admission into the team. He conveyed his delight about starting his professional career as well as his thanks for the chance.

Skenes and the Pirates organisation greeted the signing with a great deal of excitement. The Pirates were ecstatic to bring a pitcher who might anchor their rotation for years to come, a generational talent, into their farm system. Skenes, for his part, was thrilled to be a part of a team that he believed appreciated him as a person in addition to a player. The Pirates' dedication to player development and their encouraging atmosphere intrigued him.

The Pittsburgh Pirates achieved a major milestone with the signing of Paul Skenes. It conveyed their goal to use player development and the draft to assemble a competitive club. Skenes' extraordinary skill and hard ethic served as a symbol of the franchise's future and optimism for a fan base longing for a comeback to the championship.

Skenes' career with the Pirates started in the lower levels, where he kept honing his craft and enhancing his pitching repertoire. He advanced through the ranks fast, indicating that he was ready for big league baseball. His fastball dominance and lethal slider made his debut with the Pirates highly anticipated, and he lived up to the anticipation.

Skenes has established himself as one of Major League Baseball's best young pitchers in the years after he signed. His arrival has had a revolutionary effect on the Pirates, rejuvenating the squad and inspiring hope in the fan base. Paul Skenes' signing was more than just a business deal; it marked the beginning of a new chapter full of promise and possibility for the team.

CHAPTER 6: MINOR LEAGUE MASTERY: HONING HIS CRAFT

Working With Coaches and Mentors

Paul Skenes's path to baseball greatness has been greatly influenced by his tight relationship with a number of mentors and coaches who saw his extraordinary skill and supported it through all of its phases. These connections have been essential to his talent development, mental approach improvement, and cultivation of a thorough grasp of the game.

The mentoring Skenes received from his high school coaches, who saw his natural skill and promise, was very beneficial to his early growth. They pushed him to push his limits, stressed the value of basics, and developed in him a strong work ethic. Their encouragement and support set the groundwork for his success in the future.

Skenes' progress continued at the Air Force Academy under the guidance of seasoned collegiate coaches who improved his repertoire, sharpened his throwing mechanics, and pushed him to compete at a greater level. They gave him insightful information on the subtleties of the game, which improved his comprehension of pitching strategy and situational awareness.

A significant turning point in Skenes' career occurred when he transferred to Louisiana State University (LSU). His enormous talent was acknowledged by the LSU coaching staff, which was directed by Jay Johnson. They gave him a customised growth plan that addressed his areas of weakness and maximised his skills. Skenes' mechanics and pitch repertoire were greatly enhanced by pitching instructor Wes Johnson, a well-known authority on biomechanics and pitch design. Skenes's career took a dramatic turn for the better thanks to the combined efforts of the LSU coaching staff and his reaching the highest level of collegiate baseball.

Skenes benefited from the direction of seasoned instructors and mentors even after joining the Pittsburgh Pirates as a professional. He worked extensively with the Pirates coaching team, who are well-known for their proficiency in player development, to enhance his abilities, broaden his skill set, and be ready for the demands of the big leagues. To quicken his learning curve, Skenes has looked to the organisation's seasoned pitchers for mentoring, taking advantage of their expertise and experience.

Skenes has worked with mentors and coaches on projects involving more than just technical expertise. They have also assisted him in gaining the emotional and mental maturity required to succeed in the demanding world of professional baseball. They have taught him the value of resiliency, tenacity, and keeping an optimistic outlook in the face of difficulty.

Because of his dedication to lifelong learning and development, Skenes has looked outside of his team for mentors and other resources. He has studied the strategies of great pitchers throughout history, visited pitching camps and clinics, and spoke with well-known pitching specialists. His never-ending quest for information has allowed him to keep on top of trends and continuously improve as a pitcher.

It is impossible to overestimate the influence coaches and mentors had on Paul Skenes' career. Their advice, assistance, and knowledge have been crucial to his growth, helping him go from a potential prospect to one of the most powerful players in the major leagues. Skenes has shown his character and constant pursuit of greatness by his willingness to learn from, adapt to, and work with those who have gone before him.

Early Days In The Minor Leagues

The Pittsburgh Pirates selected Paul Skenes as the first overall choice in the 2023 MLB Draft, and he rose quickly through the minor league ranks. His strong pitching outings, which included a lethal slider and an overwhelming fastball that often reached triple digits, defined his climb.

Skenes signed with the Pirates and joined the Florida Complex League (FCL) Pirates in August 2023, where he made his professional debut. He displayed his exceptional velocity by striking out two hitters in a scoreless inning on his debut. Skenes had an outstanding start and quickly rose through the Pirates farm system. He went to the Double-A Altoona Curve after a short stint with the Single-A Bradenton Marauders. Despite receiving swift promotions, Skenes kept up his strong play, striking out a lot of batters and displaying his promise as a future ace.

Skenes started the 2024 season with the Indianapolis Indians of Triple-A, where he remained unstoppable. Early in his career, he had remarkable pitch control and command, which led to a run of shutout games and an outstanding strikeout percentage. He gained notoriety in April 2024 for a start in which he fired 34 pitches above 100 mph and averaged 100.5 mph on his fastball. His ability to routinely attain peak velocity was highlighted by this performance, which further cemented his standing as a top talent.

The Pirates took a careful approach to Skenes' development despite his domination, putting more stock in his long-term performance and health than in his haste to get to the big leagues. They made sure he wasn't overworked at such a young point in his career by carefully controlling his innings and pitch counts. But Skenes' unwavering domination in the 2024 season raised rumours that he would be promoted to the majors early. Fans and commentators alike were excited by his performances and were looking forward to seeing him on the stage.

Skenes had difficulties throughout his early minor league career. In Double-A, he had a little setback after having trouble controlling himself during one appearance and giving up a couple walks. But he recovered fast from this "rough" experience, showcasing his adaptability and fortitude. All things considered, Skenes' early minor league career was marked by domination, quick promotions, and a well planned development strategy meant to secure his long-term success. From the start, there was a great deal of expectation for him to make it to the main leagues because of his extraordinary skill and potential.

CHAPTER 7: MAJOR LEAGUE DEBUT

First Major League Game

A huge chapter in Paul Skenes' career opened on May 11, 2024, when he made his much awaited Major League Baseball (MLB) debut. This pitching debut against the Chicago Cubs at PNC Park was a turning point in the young pitcher's development and evidence of his quick rise through the minor league ranks.

Fans and observers alike were excited to see the top prospect in action, and there was a tangible sense of anticipation for Skenes' debut. PNC Park was rocking, with an electrifying crowd that was humming with anticipation. The excitement mounted despite a weather delay that delayed the start time, reaching a climax when Skenes took the mound for the first time as a big leaguer.

A 101 mph fastball from Skenes set the tone early in the contest. It made it clear to everyone in attendance that he was here to dominate and to display the explosive skill that had helped him advance through the minor league ranks. With a devastating slider as his follow-up, he displayed the toolkit that had made him one of the most widely anticipated prospects in recent memory.

He had a strong first inning. He showed off his calm and composure on the big stage by striking out the first two hitters he faced. He walked one batter, but he got back up fast and struck out another to close the inning. The audience cheered, realising what they were seeing had promise.

In the second inning, Skenes' control faltered a little. He let up a run and a few hits, illustrating the difficulties of adapting to life in the big leagues. To lessen the damage, he replied with his characteristic fortitude and struck out another batter. His resilience in the face of difficulty demonstrated the mental toughness that had defined his minor league career.

There was little change in the third or fourth innings. Skenes kept up his impressive performance, registering strikeouts and controlling the Cubs' offence with his blazing fastball and deadly slider. His powerful and precise performance was a showcase for his extraordinary skill and promise.

Although it wasn't perfect, Skenes' MLB debut was unquestionably noteworthy. With seven strikeouts in four innings, he demonstrated his elite level of competition in the game. He walked a few batters and gave up three runs, but these were little details in an excellent effort. He handled the pressure and expectations with grace and maturity befitting a seasoned veteran.

The actual game went back-and-forth, with the Pirates winning 10–9 in the end to claim victory. But Skenes' debut stayed front and centre. His performance gave us a sneak peek at what kind of dominating pitcher he was going to be. Fans of the Pirates and baseball in general would remember that evening for years to come.

Skenes' first MLB game served as evidence of his extraordinary skill, perseverance, and hard work. It was a triumphant moment, the result of years of planning and growth. Even though it was just one game, it signalled the start of a bright career with immense promise. That evening, when Skenes left the mound, he had not only made his Major League Baseball debut, but he had also declared himself a formidable opponent.

Getting Past Obstacles And Adversity

Paul Skenes' ascent through the minor league ranks and his much awaited MLB debut, which captivated the baseball community, constituted an incredible voyage to the major leagues. His road to success hasn't been without obstacles, however, and he has continuously surmounted them with tenacity, resolve, and unyielding mental toughness.

Skenes had a spectacular debut with the FCL Pirates, showcasing his explosive fastball and lethal slider, to start his professional career. From the beginning, he demonstrated his ability to overwhelm hitters with pitches that broke sharply and had triple digit velocity, which paved the way for his quick rise through the minor league ranks. From the FCL to Single-A, Double-A, and Triple-A, he advanced swiftly, always surpassing expectations and proving he was ready for the next level.

On May 11, 2024, he made his Major League Baseball debut against the Chicago Cubs. It was a moment of success and the result of years of training and progress. He showed his calmness and brilliance, striking out seven hitters and displaying his formidable arsenal despite a rain delay and difficult circumstances. Despite a few control problems, he had an outstanding performance that showed he could compete at the greatest level.

Following Skenes' debut, the public and media responded tremendously favourably. His performance was praised by analysts and pundits as evidence of his enormous potential, and fans voiced their delight and adoration for his lethal slider and blazing fastball. Those who supported the Pirates, who regarded him as a possible saviour for their faltering team, were filled with excitement and hope after his debut.

Skenes' path has not, however, been without difficulties. He had several early hiccups in his minor league career, including a "rough" Double-A appearance when he battled with control. When he got to the majors, he too struggled with control in his first game. These difficulties put his will to the test, but in the end they were teaching moments that accelerated his development.

Skenes is able to overcome these challenges for a number of reasons. He has a great mental game that keeps him calm and focused in stressful situations. His progress has been greatly aided by his unwavering work ethic and devotion to his art, as he is always looking to strengthen his areas of weakness and increase his strengths. In addition, he has the solid support of his teammates, coaches, family, and friends, all of whom have encouraged and mentored him along the way.

Most significantly, Skenes has a natural ability to recover from failures due to his tenacity. Instead of allowing hardship to define him, he utilises it as fuel to push himself farther and disprove those who doubt him. This perseverance has been the secret to his success and will surely continue to be important in his future career, along with his skill, work ethic, and mental toughness.

Skenes will undoubtedly run into more challenges and disappointments as his MLB career progresses. But he has the resources and mentality to overcome them because of his prior experiences. The baseball community is excited about Paul Skenes's next chapter as he continues to mature and become one of the most formidable pitchers in the league.

CHAPTER 8: LIFE OFF THE FIELD

Hobbies And Interests Outside of Baseball

Apart from his remarkable abilities in baseball, Paul Skenes has a varied range of interests and pastimes that enhance his overall well-being and enable him to enjoy a balanced existence.

Skenes' father was in the United States Air Force, therefore he has a long history with the military. It was this upbringing that gave him a great deal of respect and admiration for the military services. Despite having chosen baseball as his job, Skenes is still involved in the military community and often expresses his appreciation for their effort and devotion. He's been known to go to military installations and speak with the troops, telling them about his experiences as a professional athlete and expressing gratitude for their commitment to national security.

Skenes was a brilliant student-athlete at Louisiana State University (LSU) who performed very well in the classroom and on the baseball field before going on to play professionally. He demonstrated his dedication to academic success and a well-rounded education by pursuing a degree in finance. Skenes has made many remarks on the significance of education and how it has enriched his life, both on and off the pitch. Even though playing baseball requires a lot of time and attention, he is still dedicated to learning new things and broadening his knowledge.

Skenes likes to spend time outside participating in different activities that let him appreciate the environment and refuel. Hiking, fishing, and discovering the natural beauty of his surroundings are among his noted hobbies. He may re-establish a connection with the simpler things in life and enjoy a much-needed respite from the rigours of professional baseball via these outdoor activities.

Skenes often highlights the significance of his friendships and family ties in his life. He cherishes these connections. Whenever feasible, he likes to spend quality time with them, whether it's over dinner, outside activities, or just lounging and catching up. He gains a feeling of belonging and a solid support network from these intimate interactions, both of which are critical to his general wellbeing.

Skenes also participates in a number of community projects, using his position as a top athlete to further good deeds. He has shown his dedication to giving back to the community and aiding those in need by taking part in philanthropic events and community outreach initiatives. Skenes' charitable side demonstrates his empathy and drive to change the world outside of sports.

Skenes has a variety of pastimes and interests in addition to athletics, especially basketball and football. He appreciates the competitiveness and athleticism shown by other athletes, and he likes watching games and cheering for his favourite teams. In his spare time, he enjoys watching movies and listening to music, which he often uses as a method to decompress.

Paul Skenes is a well-rounded person who is not only characterised by his baseball career, as seen by his wide range of interests and pastimes. His varied personality is influenced by his experience in the military, intellectual endeavours, love of the outdoors, family values, and enjoyment of many kinds of entertainment. He becomes a more well-rounded and approachable person both on and off the field as a result of these off-field activities, which provide him perspective, equilibrium, and a feeling of satisfaction beyond the baseball diamond.

Community Involvement and Charity Work

Even at his early age and with a fledgling baseball career, Paul Skenes has already shown a remarkable dedication to community service and humanitarian work. He shows his compassion and willingness to give back to the community by using his position as a professional athlete to make a good difference.

Skenes has a strong affinity with the military community because of his father's Air Force service. He takes an active interest in activities and projects that aid service members and their families. He has gone to military installations, spoken to the troops, and conveyed his appreciation for their service. Additionally, he has participated in fundraising events for the USO and the Wounded Warrior Project, two groups that assist soldiers and their families.

Skenes understands the value of motivating and encouraging youth, especially those with a passion for baseball. He has shared his expertise and love of baseball with young players by taking part in youth baseball clinics and camps. Additionally, he has participated in mentoring programs where he has given advice and encouragement to young individuals who are following their goals or confronting obstacles.

His desire to interact with young people shows that he is dedicated to developing the next wave of athletes and leaders.

Skenes takes an active position in community outreach activities, concentrating on projects that tackle social concerns including healthcare, education, and poverty. He has dedicated his time to help people in need at the food banks, shelters, and hospitals in his community. Additionally, he has contributed to fund-raising campaigns for groups that support impoverished areas by offering goods and services. His enthusiastic participation in these outreach initiatives demonstrates his empathy and drive to significantly improve the lives of others.

Skenes has forged alliances with a number of nonprofit groups, endorsing their causes with his name. He has taken part in campaigns and activities aimed at generating money for these organisations by spreading awareness of their cause. Additionally, he has encouraged people to become part of their work by promoting it on social media. His efforts to use his platform for the greater good are shown by his partnerships with nonprofits.

In addition, Skenes has started his own charitable endeavours, concentrating on causes near and dear to his heart. Even while the specifics of these projects are still under wraps, it is obvious that he is dedicated to leaving a lasting impression on the neighbourhood. His readiness to devote time and money to charitable causes says volumes about his moral fibre and desire to make a good impact on the world.

Skenes's humanitarian contributions and participation in the community are evidence of his moral fibre and principles. Despite his youth and his demanding professional athletic schedule, he places a high value on improving the lives of others and giving back to the community. His commitment to humanitarian endeavours, community outreach, youth participation, military support, and charity alliances shows his compassion and generosity as well as his willingness to utilise his position for the benefit of society. It seems certain that Paul Skenes will continue to be a driving force for good change in the community even as he pursues his baseball career.

CHAPTER 9: SKENE'S LEGACY: INSPIRING THE NEXT GENERATION

Impact On Young Athletes

Beyond only his remarkable throwing ability, Paul Skenes has a profound impact on upcoming sportsmen. His story, which is full of perseverance, hard work, and unflinching faith in one's own ability, is an inspiration to aspiring athletes in many other sports.

Skenes is a great baseball role model because of his ascent to fame in the sport from collegiate star to first overall choice in the MLB draft. His story exemplifies the value of persistence, hard effort, and unflinching confidence. Young athletes see him as an example of how dreams may come true if they are dedicated and persistent enough. His remarkable work ethic, humility, and dedication to lifelong learning serve as a beacon of hope for young people aspiring to be the best in their chosen sports.

Beyond the tangible side of athletics, Skenes, an LSU finance graduate, aggressively promotes the value of education in addition to athletic endeavours. He exhorts young players to put their academic growth first because he understands the importance of a well-rounded education in creating great people off the field as well as on. Through his support of education, he encourages young athletes to tackle their academic objectives with the same fervour and commitment they give to their sport, resulting in a more comprehensive approach to personal growth.

Skenes' dedication to living a healthy lifestyle increases the good effects of his influence. Being a professional athlete, he is aware of how important it is to have a healthy lifestyle. He emphasises the value of healthy behaviours in maximising athletic performance and general well-being, such as appropriate diet, consistent exercise, and enough sleep. His commitment to a healthy lifestyle serves as an example for young athletes, who are inspired to focus their physical and mental well-being and make wise decisions.

Skenes regularly participates in community outreach with young athletes by running baseball clinics, camps, and mentorship programs, among other things. Aspiring athletes may get crucial insights and assistance from him by sharing his expertise and experience. His contacts with young people not only serve as an inspiration to them, but also provide them with the resources and skills necessary to excel in life and in their chosen sport.

Although Skenes' path has not been without difficulties and disappointments, his capacity to triumph over misfortune provides young sportsmen with a valuable lesson. Throughout his career, he has encountered challenges, but he has always overcome them with resiliency and willpower. His narrative emphasises to young athletes the value of mental toughness, tenacity, and an optimistic outlook when confronted with obstacles, highlighting the fact that failures are just stepping stones on the road to achievement.

Pitcher Skenes is aware of the value of collaboration and leadership in attaining success. On the field, he continuously exemplifies these traits by cooperating with his colleagues to accomplish shared objectives. Young athletes are inspired by his leadership style and focus on teamwork, which teaches them the importance of cooperation, respect for one another, and communication in reaching group goals.

Paul Skenes' influence on aspiring players extends beyond the baseball diamond. Young people from diverse backgrounds may relate to his tale, which encourages them to follow their goals with tenacity, enthusiasm, and perseverance. Young athletes look up to him as a role model because he shows them the value of perseverance, hard effort, education, healthy living, and community involvement. His ability to positively impact youth is evidence of his moral fibre, principles, and dedication to changing the world.

Inspiring Others To Pursue Their Dreams

The story of Paul Skenes' ascent to the major leagues is not just one of physical achievement but also one of tenacity, diligence, and a steadfast trust in one's own abilities. For many people who want to be the best in their areas, his tale is a source of inspiration and optimism.

Skene's ascent from a collegiate athlete to the first overall choice in the MLB draft is a perfect example of the American Dream. Regardless of their upbringing or situation, anyone who dares to dream large may relate to his story. His accomplishments encourage people to pursue greatness and have faith in their own abilities despite whatever challenges they may encounter.

Skenes' success comes from numerous hours of effort, devotion, and unshakable commitment to his craft; it's not just the outcome of innate skill. He is a live example of how great accomplishments may be attained through perseverance and hard effort. His narrative inspires people to rise to the challenge, reach new heights, and never give up on their goals.

His path has not been without its share of difficulties and disappointments. Throughout his career, he has had difficulties, but he has always overcome them, displaying tenacity and mental toughness. His capacity for overcoming challenges encourages people to tackle challenges head-on, learn from mistakes, and come out stronger after each setback.

His dedication to learning is shown by his finance degree from LSU, which emphasises the value of having a well-rounded outlook on life. He advises people to pursue their studies in addition to their hobbies, especially those who want to be sports. His academic accomplishments show that it is possible to succeed in many facets of life and that obtaining a degree may lead to a wealth of new options.

Skenes regularly interacts with youth via a range of community-based activities, including camps, baseball clinics, and mentorship schemes. He gives people courage to follow their aspirations by imparting his wisdom, insights, and experiences. Aspiring athletes and those looking to have a good influence on their communities may benefit greatly from his coaching and advice. Skenes' tale is one of inspiration, optimism, and unwavering dream-chasing. He is the epitome of tenacity, showing that everything is achievable with effort, commitment, and a resolute conviction in oneself. People from all walks of life can relate to his path and are motivated to pursue their goals with unrelenting enthusiasm and tenacity.

The influence of Paul Skenes goes far beyond the baseball field. He is more than simply an athlete; he is a monument to the strength of the human spirit, a symbol of inspiration, and a source of hope. His narrative serves as a helpful reminder that aspirations are real, attainable objectives that can be reached with perseverance, hard effort, and unshakeable faith in oneself. Skenes' legacy will surely encourage numerous people to follow their aspirations with newfound zeal and dedication as he continues his career, creating an enduring impression on the sports world and beyond.

CONCLUSION

The Enduring Legacy of a Rising Star

Even though Paul Skenes' professional career is still in its early stages, his long reputation as a rising star in baseball is already starting to take form. His influence on the game goes beyond his outstanding accomplishments and stats; it also includes the motivation he offers to aspiring sportsmen, the enthusiasm he arouses in spectators, and the possibility that he may completely alter the definition of a pitcher in the contemporary game.

A Beacon of Hope: Skenes' transformation from a gifted high school athlete to a dominating university player and the first overall draft choice offers hope to all aspiring athletes. His narrative is a powerful example of the value of commitment, perseverance, and unflinching self-belief. He is the embodiment of the notion that great things can be accomplished with the correct attitude, a strong support network, and unceasing work.

Defining the Position of the Pitcher: The conventional ideas of what a pitcher can be is challenged by Skenes' exceptional combination of stature, agility, velocity, and command. The expectations placed on current pitchers have completely changed due to his ability to regularly hurl fastballs in the triple digits while retaining perfect control. He is a complete athlete who personifies the advancement of the position, not just a powerful pitcher.

Motivating a New Generation: Skenes has enthralled baseball fans and motivated a new generation of players with his exciting mound appearances. Young athletes have found inspiration in his love for the game, his unrelenting spirit of competition, and his modest manner, which inspires them to aim high and follow their ambitions with unyielding commitment.

A Catalyst for Change: Skenes' entry into the big leagues might spur changes in both the Pittsburgh Pirates club and the game at large. The Pirates fan base is excited and full of hope again because of his arrival, and they can't wait to see the club succeed again. His on-field performance has the power to spur his colleagues to greater heights and improve the team's overall performance.

A Legacy in the Making: Skenes' influence on the game is already evident, despite the fact that his career is still in its early phases. Due to his accomplishments on and off the field, he has gained the respect and adoration of rivals as well as fans. Not only are his accomplishments and accolades what define his legacy, but also the inspiration he brings, the transformation he sparks, and the long-lasting influence he has on the game.

Skenes' legacy will develop and grow even while he pursues his career goals. He has the ability to win a World Series, be a Cy Young Award winner, and be a consistent All-Star. His influence on baseball may stretch beyond his playing career as he might serve as an inspiration to future pitchers and further the sport's continuous development.

Paul Skenes's lasting legacy is a tale of inspiration, optimism, and the unwavering quest of greatness. This narrative serves as a powerful reminder of the value of hard effort, the strength of aspirations, and the constancy of self-belief. We can be certain that his influence on the game will last for many years as we see the next chapter of his incredible career.

Made in the USA
Coppell, TX
29 November 2024

41348864R00056